Sea Urchins

Meryl Magby

PowerKiDS
press.

New York

For my niece, Teagan Parker

Published in 2013 by The Rosen Publishing Group, Inc.
29 East 21st Street, New York, NY 10010

First Edition

Editor: Amelie von Zumbusch
Book Design: Greg Tucker

Photo Credits: Cover, pp. 5, 8, 9 (top, bottom) 17 Shutterstock.com; p. 4 iStockphoto/Thinkstock; pp. 6–7 Stuart Westmorland/Photodisc/Getty Images; p. 10 AbleStock.com/Thinkstock; p. 11 © www.iStockphoto.com/microgen; pp. 12–13 Joe Dovala/WaterFrame/Getty Images; p. 14 liquidlibrary/Thinkstock; p. 16 Hemera/Thinkstock; p. 18 Paul Nicklen/National Geographic/Getty Images; p. 19 Visuals Unlimited/Wim van Egmond/Getty Images; p. 20 David Courtenay/Oxford Scientific/Getty Images; p. 21 Jonathan Bird/Peter Arnold/Getty Images; p. 22 ©www.iStockphoto.com/Extreme-Photographer.

Library of Congress Cataloging-in-Publication Data

Magby, Meryl.
 Sea urchins / by Meryl Magby. — 1st ed.
    p. cm. — (Under the sea)
 ISBN 978-1-4488-7400-2 (library binding) — ISBN 978-1-4488-7479-8 (pbk.) —
 ISBN 978-1-4488-7553-5 (6-pack)

 1. Sea urchins—Juvenile literature. I. Title.
 QL384.E2M26 2013
 593.9'5—dc23
                                                       2011049572

Manufactured in China

CPSIA Compliance Information: Batch #WKTS12PK: For Further Information contact Rosen Publishing, New York, New York at 1-800-237-9932

Contents

Moving Pincushions

Sea urchins are small underwater animals that look like pincushions. Their round bodies are covered with sharp **spines**. However, sea urchins do not sit still, as pincushions do. These amazing animals can move across the ocean floor. They even climb up rocks!

Like sea urchins, sand dollars are found in waters around the world.

There are more than 700 kinds of sea urchins. Purple sea urchins live along the eastern shores of the Pacific Ocean.

Sea urchins are **invertebrates**. This means they do not have backbones. They are closely related to sand dollars. They are also related to sea stars and sea cucumbers. Sea urchins and their relatives have been around for a very long time. The earliest animals related to sea urchins **evolved** about 450 million years ago.

Digging Holes for Homes

Sea urchins are found in all of Earth's oceans. They can live in cold water or warm water. Some sea urchins live in very shallow water near the coast. Others live in somewhat deeper water farther from shore.

Sea urchins like to burrow, or dig holes, halfway into sand, mud, and rocks. This helps sea urchins stay safe from ocean waves and currents. Sea urchins also like to live where they can find food. These places include coral reefs, kelp forests, and sea grass beds. Many sea urchins live in coral reefs around Hawaii, Australia, and islands in the Caribbean Sea.

These long-spined sea urchins live in the warm waters around Negros Oriental Island, in the Philippines.

Many Sharp Spines

Sea urchins have round bodies. A sea urchin's body gets its shape from a hard outer skeleton, called a test. The test is covered with hundreds of sharp movable spines. Long thin tubes, called tube feet, stretch out between the spines. Tube feet help sea urchins move and catch food. Sea urchins breathe through their tube feet. Sea urchins also

Sea urchin tests are made of many hard plates. These plates lock together tightly to make a solid skeleton.

Top: Sea urchins can be many colors. *Right:* This is a dried sea urchin test. You can sometimes find dried tests washed up on beaches.

have many tiny **pincer** arms. The pincers work to keep their bodies clean.

Sea urchins' mouths are on the bottoms of their bodies. A sea urchin's mouth has five teeth that help it break down food.

Sea Urchin Senses

Sea urchins have a good sense of touch. If something touches a sea urchin's body, it will point all of its spines toward that part of its body.

Sea urchins do not have real eyes, as people and many other animals do. However, sea urchins do

If you pick up a sea urchin, be careful. Their spines can be very sharp and some can sting you!

Scientists have found that urchins with more tightly packed spines sense light better than those with spines that are farther apart.

sense light. At the back of a human eye, there is a special **tissue** that reacts to light. This tissue is called a retina. Although sea urchins do not have eyes, they have special **cells** that act like retinas. Most of these cells are found on a sea urchin's tube feet. Scientists think that they let sea urchins see!

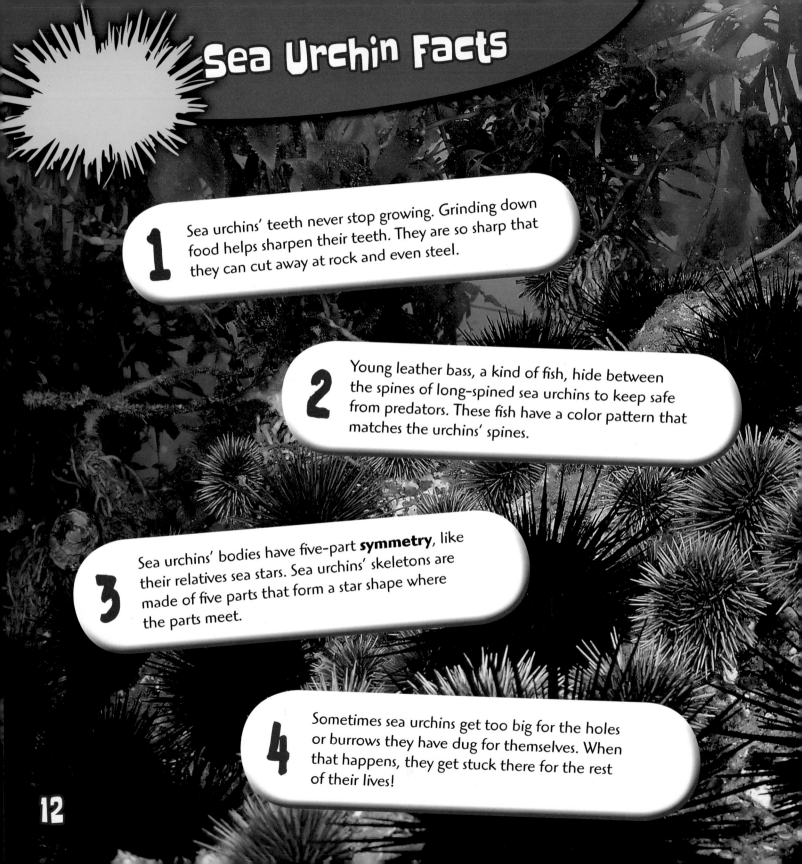

Sea Urchin Facts

1 Sea urchins' teeth never stop growing. Grinding down food helps sharpen their teeth. They are so sharp that they can cut away at rock and even steel.

2 Young leather bass, a kind of fish, hide between the spines of long-spined sea urchins to keep safe from predators. These fish have a color pattern that matches the urchins' spines.

3 Sea urchins' bodies have five-part **symmetry**, like their relatives sea stars. Sea urchins' skeletons are made of five parts that form a star shape where the parts meet.

4 Sometimes sea urchins get too big for the holes or burrows they have dug for themselves. When that happens, they get stuck there for the rest of their lives!

5 Paying attention to sea urchins is a good way to tell whether ocean water is becoming polluted. Sea urchins living in polluted water often have drooping spines and stop moving.

6 Young purple sea urchins have green spines, not purple ones!

7 Sea otters that eat purple sea urchins are easy to recognize. This is because these otters often have purple teeth. Sometimes their bones even turn purple!

8 Sea urchins that live in shallow water often cover their bodies with shells, rocks, and pieces of **algae**. Scientists think they do this to keep themselves from drying out or being eaten by seabirds.

Moving in Groups

Some kinds of sea urchins that live in very shallow water along the coast live alone. However, sea urchins that live in deeper waters tend to live in large groups. These groups move across the ocean floor slowly, eating as they go. The urchins in these groups often feed on sea grasses or kelp forests.

Sea urchins move across the ocean floor with the help of their movable spines. The hundreds of short spines on the bottom of an urchin's body act like legs. The urchins' tube feet also let them climb up rocks and stick to the ocean floor.

Purple sea urchins, such as these, live in big groups.

Finding Food

Sea urchins eat both plants and animals. Some sea urchins wait for bits of algae, sea grass, or dead animals to float by. Urchins that move in large groups can eat entire kelp forests. This can leave other small ocean animals that make kelp forests their homes with no place to live and no food to eat.

You can see a sea urchin's five teeth in this close-up photo.

Sea urchins spear food with their sharp spines. The tube feet on the top of a sea urchin's body can also grab food as it is floating by. Then, the tube feet work together to pass the food to the sea urchin's mouth on the bottom of its body.

Male and female sea urchins look exactly the same. However, they have different **reproductive organs**. Sea urchins reproduce outside their bodies. First, female sea urchins release millions of tiny eggs into the water. Then, sperm released

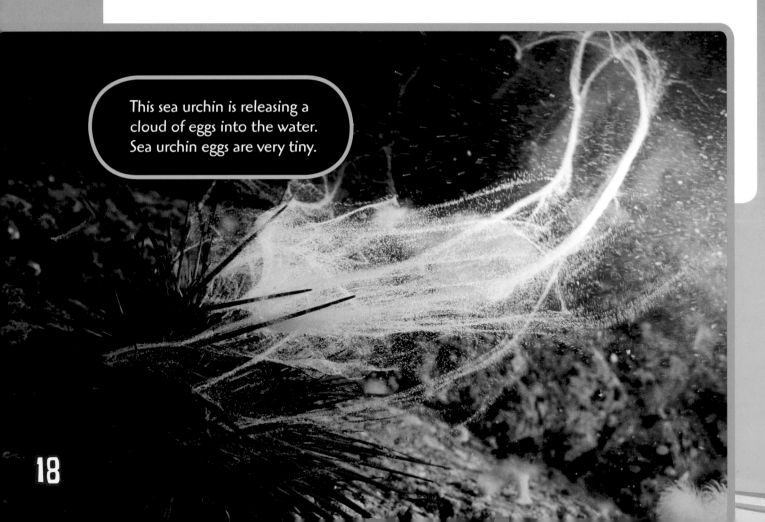

This sea urchin is releasing a cloud of eggs into the water. Sea urchin eggs are very tiny.

18

This is the larva of a common heart urchin. These sea urchins are also known as sea potatoes.

by male sea urchins **fertilizes** the eggs. The fertilized eggs become **larvae**.

Sea urchin larvae swim to the water's surface. There, they eat tiny animals called phytoplankton. After several weeks, the larvae start to grow the body parts of an adult urchin and sink to the ocean floor. Sea urchins are old enough to reproduce when they are about two to five years old.

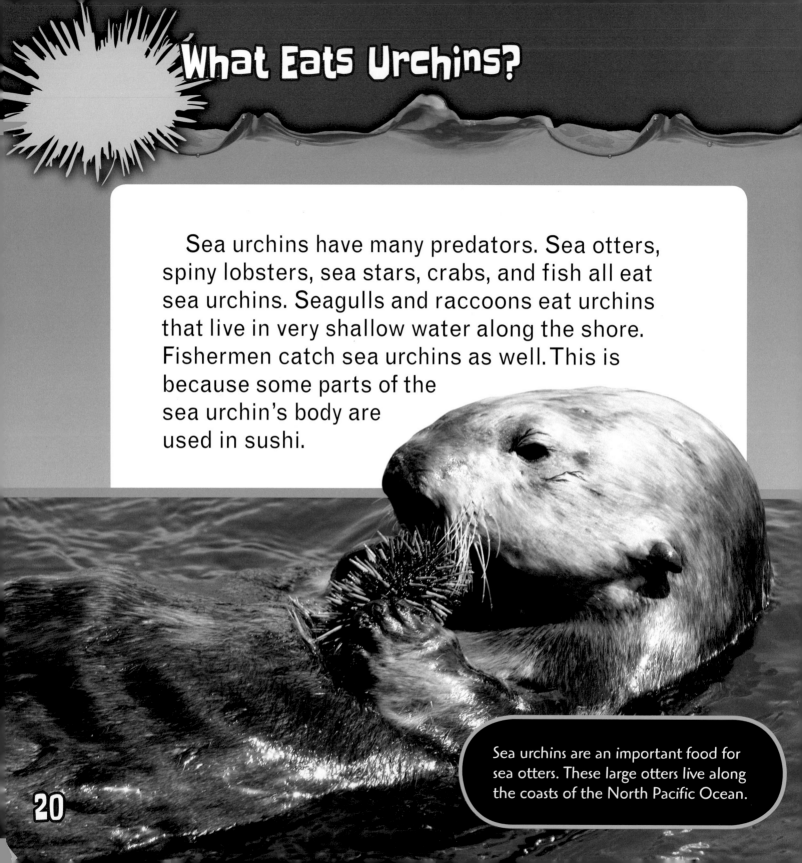

What Eats Urchins?

Sea urchins have many predators. Sea otters, spiny lobsters, sea stars, crabs, and fish all eat sea urchins. Seagulls and raccoons eat urchins that live in very shallow water along the shore. Fishermen catch sea urchins as well. This is because some parts of the sea urchin's body are used in sushi.

Sea urchins are an important food for sea otters. These large otters live along the coasts of the North Pacific Ocean.

Sea urchins try to keep safe from animal predators by hiding during the day. Their sharp spines keep many predators from getting too close. The spines of some urchins even contain **venom**. Venom can make other animals sick or die.

The Right Number

Sea urchins play a big role in many ocean **food webs**. Food webs are groups of living things that depend on each other for food.

There can sometimes be too many sea urchins. When urchins eat all the food in one area, it leaves nothing for other animals to eat! At other times, fishermen catch too many sea urchins. Urchins die from ocean pollution, too. Then, the urchins' predators have nothing to eat. Taking care of the ocean helps make sure that there is the right number of sea urchins!

This scuba diver found a sea urchin! Scuba divers are people who wear special gear to look at things that live underwater.

Glossary

algae (AL-jee) Plantlike living things without roots or stems that live in water.

cells (SELZ) The basic units of living things.

evolved (ih-VOLVD) Changed over many years.

fertilizes (FUR-tuh-lyz-ez) Puts male cells inside an egg to make babies.

food webs (FOOD WEBZ) Living things that depend on each other for food.

invertebrates (in-VER-teh-brets) Animals without backbones.

larvae (LAHR-vee) Animals in an early period of life.

pincer (PIN-sur) A sharp claw.

reproductive organs (ree-pruh-DUK-tiv OR-genz) The body parts inside an animal that allow it to make babies.

spines (SPYNZ) Sharp, pointy things.

symmetry (SIH-muh-tree) Being equal on all sides.

tissue (TIH-shoo) Something that forms the parts of living things.

venom (VEH-num) A poison passed by one animal into another through a bite or a sting.

Index

Websites

Due to the changing nature of Internet links, PowerKids Press has developed an online list of websites related to the subject of this book. This site is updated regularly. Please use this link to access the list: www.powerkidslinks.com/uts/urch/